James Haar

The Tugendsterne of Harsdörffer and Staden

AMERICAN INSTITUTE OF MUSICOLOGY

ARMEN CARAPETYAN, Ph. D.
DIRECTOR

MUSICOLOGICAL STUDIES AND DOCUMENTS

14

JAMES HAAR

THE TUGENDSTERNE OF HARSDÖRFFER AND STADEN
AN EXERCISE IN MUSICAL HUMANISM

MUSICOLOGICAL STUDIES AND DOCUMENTS

14

JAMES HAAR

THE TUGENDSTERNE OF HARSDÖRFFER AND STADEN

AN EXERCISE IN MUSICAL HUMANISM

AMERICAN INSTITUTE OF MUSICOLOGY

1965

INTRODUCTION

In the humanistic world, that pleasant grove of Academe where Renaissance scholars, crossing themselves perfunctorily as they entered, dreamed their beautiful dreams of antique life and culture, music was given an honored, but usually a rather vague, role to play. It is true that despite the absence of any tangible models, some efforts were made at imitating ancient Greek music; [1] but for the most part Renaissance writers were content to rehearse the paraphernalia of myth and speculation which surrounds the music of classical antiquity, paying the most graceful compliments to an art which they doubtless thought of in the most shockingly anachronistic terms. So the legion of myths about the powers of music, commanded by Orpheus with Arion and Amphion as prominent subalterns, passed in more or less disciplined array through the pages of encyclopaedists [2] and of musical theorists. [3] So too the great Platonic-Pythagorean notions of the harmonious universe, always honored in the canonic statement of Boethius,

[1] A summary of the most important of these attempts may be seen in D. P. Walker, "Musical Humanism in the 16th and Early 17th Centuries", *Music Review* II (1941), pp. 1-13; 111-121; 220-227; 288-308; III (1942), pp. 55-71.

[2] See, for example, the bewildering collection of myths in Giorgio Valla's *De Expetendis et Fugiendis Rebus Opus* (Venice, 1501), in I, i, of the *De Musica* section.

[3] The opening chapter of Gafori's *Theorica musicae* (1480) is an early, rather disorderly example. More systematic collections of classical myths may be seen in 16th-century theorists, Zarlino being a good example.

were revived and most enthusiastically embroidered by fifteenth- and sixteenth-century Platonists. [4] And the supposed part music could play in astrological theory and pratice was elaborated by Ficino, [5] by Cornelius Agrippa, [6] then by later followers of these men.

Before long classical lore about music had become standard household information in educated circles; this is seen in works like the *Courtier*, [7] and is confirmed by the fact that musical games of humanistic character were played by members of sixteenth-century Italian academies [8] and, later, by their counterparts north of the Alps. [9] Both musical myths and the Platonic *harmonia mundi* served as themes for the numerous intermedi, ballets, and masques which graced so many Renaissance weddings, entries, and other occasions of state. The ambitious

[4] A particularly imaginative restatement of the whole doctrine of *musica mundana* can be found in the first dialogue of the *De Musica* of Giorgio Anselmi, a work called to the attention of musicologists by Jacques Handschin (see his "Anselmi's Treatise on Music Annotated by Gafori", *Musica Disciplina* II (1948), pp. 123-140). Anselmi's work is now to be seen in a modern edition: *Georgii Anselmi Parmensis De Musica,* ed. G. Massera. "Historiae Musicae Cultores" Biblioteca XIV. (Florence: Olschki, 1961). See especially pp. 97-106 of this edition.

[5] For Ficino's astrological music, and that of some of his followers, see D. P. Walker, *Spiritual and Demonic Magic from Ficino to Campanella* (London: The Warburg Insitute, 1958).

[6] In Book II, ch. 24-26 of his *Occulta philosophia.* See Vol. I, pp. 312-321 of the French translation of the work, by F. Gaboriau Paris, 1910).

[7] In the first book. See pp. 74-77 in the translation of C. S. Singleton (New York: Doubleday, 1959).

[8] In the *Centi Giuochi Liberali et d'ingegno* (Bologna, 1551) of Innocenzio Ringhieri, there is an amusingly pedantic *giuoco della musica* (IX, pp. 143r—144v). See J. Haar, "On Musical Games in the 16th Century", *Journal of the American Musicological Society* XV (1962) pp. 22-34.

[9] Harsdörffer has a *spiel* on music; see below, and note 29.

tableaux musicaux invented by Count Giovanni de' Bardi for the wedding of Ferdinando de' Medici in 1589 included a realization of Plato's myth of Er, with its singing Sirens; the Pythic contest of Apollo; and the story of Arion and the dolphin. [10] Many other examples of fêtes employing classical musical themes could be quoted; they seem, for instance, to have been popular at the court of Louis XIII. In 1628 a *Ballet de la cour de Soleil*, which included a Boethian dance of planets and seasons, was performed; at Paris in 1632 a *Balet de l'Harmonie* showed its audience Apollo, Orpheus, Venus, the Graces, and even a personification of the six „notes" (the hexachord?) of music. [11] As in the poetry of Elizabethan and Stuart England, references to classical musical subjects, particularly those dealing with *musica mundana*, seem to have multiplied towards the end of the Renaissance, at a time when belief in the neo-Platonic cosmos and its music had faded, becoming graceful metaphor and nothing more. [12]

Eclectic Neo-Platonism; the intermedio, ballet, or mas-

[10] The most complete description of the Florentine *intermedi* of 1589 is by A. Warburg, "I costumi teatrali per gli intermezzi del 1589", *Gesammelte Schriften* (Leipzig, 1932), I, pp. 259-300. For the music, printed in part in Max Schneider's *Die Anfänge des Basso Continuo* (Leipzig, 1918), pp. 116-157, see D. P. Walker, "La musique des intermèdes florentins de 1589 et l'humanisme", *Les Fêtes de la Renaissance*, ed. J. Jacquot (Paris: Centre National de la Recherche Scientifique, 1956), pp. 133-144. A complete edition of the music, by Mr. Walker, has now appeared: *Les fêtes de Florence (1589). Musique des intermèdes de "La Pellegrina"* (Paris: Centre National de la Recherche Scientifique, 1963).

[11] See P. Lacroix, *Ballets et Mascarades de cour de Henri II à Louis XIV*. 6 vols. (Geneva, 1868-70), III, pp. 207-219, for the *Balet de l'Harmonie*. The *Ballet de la cour de Soleil* is mentioned by F. Yates, *The French Academies of the 16th Century* (London, 1947), p. 270. No music is known to survive for either of these ballets.

[12] On this tendency as seen in English poetry John Hollander's *The Untuning of the Skies* (Princeton, 1961) is useful.

que; the playfully intellectual parlor game — all these are elements in the little musical pageant *Die Tugendsterne* of the Nürnberg academician Georg Philipp Harsdörffer (1607-1658) and his musical collaborator Sigmund Theophil Staden (1607-1655). In this work the planets sing, and we are given, in rather *heimlich* style, the music of the spheres. These stars affect human life, and thus astrology enters; but the planets are Virtues as well, with strongly pietistic Christian coloring. Nonetheless the trappings of these Planet-Virtues are those taken from alchemical and astrological lore, through the intermediary of the aristocratic science of heraldry. [13] The result is a quite fascinating bit of musical humanism made literal. If the reader's curiosity is aroused he is urged to turn now to the translation and transcription of *Die Tugendsterne* at the end of this account; or, if he can wait, to look at it after he has followed the present account of Harsdörffer's sources and methods. [13a].

In his lifelong effort to bring to German readers what he considered best in Italian, Spanish, French, and English literature and custom, Harsdörffer [14] translated or adapted an amazing amount of material, turning to the novella,

[13] For connections between alchemy, astrology, and heraldry see John Read, *Prelude to Chemistry* (New York, 1937), p. 92.

[13a] A somewhat less detailed account of the *Tugendsterne* may be found in J. Haar, "Astral Music in Seventeenth-century Nuremberg: the Tugendsterne of Harsdörffer and Staden", *Musica Disciplina* XVI (1962), pp. 175-189.

[14] The fullest biography of Harsdörffer is that of Theodore Bischoff, *Georg Philipp Harsdörffer, Ein Zeitbild aus dem 17. Jahrhundert,* in the *Festschrift zur 250-jährigen Jubelfeier des Pegnesischen Blumenordens in Nürnberg* (Nürnberg, 1894). An earlier study of Harsdörffer and some fellow poets, J. Tittman's *Die Nürnberger Dichterschule: Harsdörffer, Klaj, Birken* (Göttingen, 1847), is still useful, as is the more specialized study of A. Krapp,, *Die ästhetischen Tendenzen Harsdörffers* (Berlin, 1903).

to drama, to poetry, to didactic works, or to literary games, as his fancy led him. His chief work, the eight-volume *Frauenzimmer-Gesprächspiele*[15] of 1641-49, is full of such translations and adaptations, containing in addition marginal notes and references which show wide reading, the bulk of it in sixteenth-century humanistic tomes (proud of his erudition, Harsdörffer even includes a bibliography of his sources in the *Gesprächspiele*[16]). The contents of the work have been analyzed in some detail,[17] but Harsdörffer seems to have worked harder than his critics, for there is still much gold to be mined from the *Gesprächspiele*, its small fat oblong volumes each offering instruction, edification, and amusement for the sympathetic reader.

Something of the musical content of the *Gesprächspiele* has been known to modern readers since Robert Eitner[18] reprinted the „opera" *Seelewig* which appears in the fourth volume of the work. *Seelewig*, a „geistliche Waldgedicht"

[15] The full title is

> Frauenzimmer Gesprechspiele/ so bey Ehr- und Tugendliebenden Gesellschaften/ mit nutzlicher Ergetzlichkeit/ beliebet und geübet werden mögen/ Aus Italiänischen/ Frantzösischen und Spanischen Scribenten angewiesen/ und jetzund ausführlicher auf sechs Personen gerichtet/ und mit einer neuer Zugabe gemehret/ Durch Einen Mitgenossen der Hochlöblichen Fruchtbringenden Gesellschaft. Nürnberg. Gedruckt und verlegt bey Wolffgang Endtner.

This is the title of the second edition, which came out in the years 1644-49. A first edition of vols. 1 and 2 appeared in 1641. The copy I have used is that of the Harvard College Library. My thanks are due to the staff of the Houghton Library at Harvard for their kind cooperation.

[16] At the end of Vol. II there is a "Register etlicher Scribenten" giving many of Harsdörffer's sources, and there is a supplement to this at the end of the fourth volume.

[17] See G. A. Narciss, *Studien zu den Frauenzimmergesprächspiele Georg Philipp Harsdörffers* (1607-1658) (Leipzig, 1928), the most thorough study of the work.

[18] R. Eitner, "Seelewig, das älteste bekannte deutsche Singspiel von Harsdörffer u. S. G. Staden 1644. Neudruck", *Monatshefte für Musik-Geschichte* XIII (1881), pp. 55-147.

set „gesangweis auf Italienische Art" [19] by Sigmund Staden, [20] son of the well-known Nürnberg musician Johann Staden, gives a good idea of the collaborative efforts of Harsdörffer and Staden (who apparently wrote all the music in the *Gesprächspiele*), but it by no means exhausts the joint musical offerings of the two. A shorter musical play from the third volume was printed in Eugen Schmitz's study [21] of the work; there still remain, however, a number of small pieces, chiefly strophic songs, scattered through the volumes, and there are many references to music, usually in humanistic vein but sometimes of a more practical nature. Some of these can be discussed here since they form a background for the *Tugendsterne*.

[19] As the title-page of the work, quoted by Eitner, *op. cit.*, p. 65, decribes *Seelewig*.

[20] For Sigmund Staden see W. Nagel, "Zur Biographie Joh. Staden's und seiner Söhne", *MfMG* XXIX (1897), pp. 53-61; cf. E. Schmitz's introduction to his edition of the works of Johann Staden in *DDT*, 2. Folge, Jahrg. 7, Band 1, pp. ixff. (Schmitz planned to edit the works of Sigmund Staden for the Bayern Denkmäler, but never did so). For Staden's output see Eitner, *Q-L*, IX, pp. 240-241. Staden was a *stadtpfeiffer* and, along with his father, a member of a musical society or academy in Nürnberg, one whose meetings the young Harsdörffer attended; see A. Sandberger, "Die Nürnberger Musikgesellschaft (1588-1629)", *MfMG* XXVI (1895), pp. 1-12. Staden was not, however, admitted to the academy Harsdörffer helped to found, the *Blumenorden an der Pegnitz;* the musician's place seems to have been that of hired help rather than of friend and equal, even though Harsdörffer praised Staden highly (in the "Erinnerung" of the fourth volume, p. cviii, he says that Staden, whom he calls "hochberühmten und kunsterfahrenen", seems born to compose).

[21] E. Schmitz, "Zur musikgeschichtlichen Bedeutung der Harsdörfferschen 'Frauenzimmergesprächspiele'," *Festschrift zum 90. Geburtstag Rochus Freiherrn von Liliencron* (Leipzig, 1910), pp. 254-277 Schmitz reprinted (pp. 264ff), the music of *Von der Welt Eitelkeit* from Vol. III, pp. 171ff. He mentions (p. 276) that of the remaining inedited music in the *Gesprächspiele* the *Tugendsterne* is the most important, but he gives no analysis of it.

Among the classical myths retold in the course of the *Gesprächspiele* (often with a moralizing Christian interpretation added) there are a few in which music has a part. The story of Arion — his lyre, and his miraculous preservation by a musically susceptible dolphin — is told at some length, [22] with two of the interlocutors of the *Gesprächspiele* announcing that they will sing of the powers of music as seen in Arion's tale. [23] Unfortunately no music is included here. Sigmund Staden was not afraid, however, to illustrate classical material with artless *lieder*; at one point a discussion [24] of the sun's yearly course and the seasons it produces brings to Harsdörffer's mind the classicizing analogy of the seasons with the vocal ranges, [25] and four of the conversationalists sing in turn of the seasons, their voices illustrating one of the analogies contained in Boethian *musica mundana.* [26] These songs will give some idea of how Staden rose to meet the Boethian challenge: [27]

[22] As *spiel* ccxxviii, pp. 29-38 of Vol. VI.

[23] The tale of Arion begins thus: "Mein Sinn erfreuet sich den Singer zu besingen, Der durch der Leyren Klang die Wellen können zwingen".

[24] *Spiel* xcv, "Vom halben Umbkreis", pp. 277-290 of Vol. II.

[25] The ancient analogy, which compares the seasons in their relationships to each other with musical consonances, may be found in Aristides Quintilianus (see pp. 343-4 of R. Schäfke's translation, *Aristeides Quintilianus von der Musik*, Berlin, 1937), in Plutarch, etc. A Renaissance version of this is in Gafori's *De Harmonia Musicorum Instrumentorum* (Milan, 1518), IV, 19, f. lxxxxviii. More common is the comparison of voices or lyre-strings to the four elements (cf. Zarlino, *Ist. Harm.* III, 58), which Harsdörffer does get to; see below, and note 30.

[26] Cf. *De institutione musica* I, ii, p. 187 Friedlein: "Et primum ea, quae est mundana, in his maxime perspicienda est, quae in ipso caelo vel compage elementorum vel temporum varietate visuntur".

[27] Only the first verse of these strophic songs is given here, since the full text adds nothing important to the present discussion.

Example 1

Lob des Frühlings

Ober-Stimme (Diskantus) allein zu singen

[Cassandra]

Example 2

Lob des Sommers

Nechst Oberstimme (Altus) allein zu singen

[Angelica]

(Whole top voice written a third too low)

Example 3

Lob des Herbsts

Gemein oder Nechstunterstimme (Tenor) allein zu singen

[Degenwert]

* The 3 sign is taken here to indicate a $\frac{3}{1}$ proportional change; in some other places $\frac{3}{2}$ seems a more just change. In neither interpretation need the tempo change be mathematically exact. I apologize for the inconsistent interpretation of the sign 3; but since this sign is not unequivocally clear it seemed best to interpret it according to the character of the pieces in which it occurs.

Example 4

Lob des Winters

Grund- oder Unterstimme (Bassus) allein zu singen

[Reymund]

The learned conversationalists of the *Gesprächspiele* are musicians as well; so the six[28] of them, to whom the reader should by this time have been introduced, are depicted in a group portrait at the beginning of the eighth volume (Plate I). Their names, illustrative of Harsdörffer's tendency to fit in edifying symbolism wherever he can, are as follows:

[28] In the first edition of the work, which I have not used, there are only four speakers. Cf. Curt von Faber du Faur, *German Baroque Literature. A Catalogue of the Collection in the Yale University Library* (New Haven, 1958), p. 135: "The first two volumes appeared in 1641, in normal octavo, and with only four participants in the dialogue, as well as without the Zugabe. The definitive form of the work appears first in the second edition of these volumes".

Plate I

Degenwert von Ruhmekk, ein verständiger und gelehrter Soldat
Cassandra Schönleben, eine Adeliche Jungfrau
Reymund Discretin, ein gereist und belesener Student [in later volumes a "hofjunker"; the chief of the panelists and the performer of the *Tugendsterne* songs]
Angelica von Keuschewitz, eine Adeliche Jungfrau
Vespasian von Lustgau, ein alter Hofmann
Julia von Freudenstein, eine Kluge Matron

The songs on the seasons lead into a *spiel* [29] on music, in which the panelists must stand or sit in obedience to a musical beat or, if they fail to do so, answer some humanistic questions about music. The questions (among them, What is the source of music: birds, waterfalls, or hammers at a smithy? What is the meaning of the Siren's tale? Is musical sound rounded, like spreading circles in water? Can music be compared to love? How can music drive away sorrow or lighten work?) are ones typical of the *laus musicae* tradition; they are not answered directly, but Vespasian, into whose mouth words of wisdom are often put, goes from them to a general reflection on the Boethian songs. Pleased that the correspondence of voices to seasons was observed, he adds that the wondrous effects of music rise from its precise analogy to the four elements: [30]

> Our life is but a sort of artful music made up of a harmony of unequal things. [31] One part of it is subtle as the life-spirit, the discant, and fire; another portion,

[29] Spiel xcvi, pp. 290-294 of Vol. II.
[30] II, pp. 293-4.
[31] This is the old Pythagorean dictum, often ascribed to Philolaus: "Harmonia est discordia concors".

somewhat more substantial, like blood, the alto, and air. Further, flesh corresponds with the tenor and with water; then, finally, bones correspond with the bass and with earth. These similarities, to my way of thinking, are responsible for the universal sympathy of men and things with music, which is a foretaste of the eternal life of the blessed.

The harmony of seasons and of elements, two parts of the Boethian *musica mundana,* have now been touched on; its principal ingredient, the harmony of the planets, will be found in the *Tugendsterne.* In the form of the choral dance of the stars Harsdörffer mentions planetary harmony several times: the first song of *Von der Welt Eitelkeit* begins with the words "Die Morgenroth bin ich, folg nach den Sternen Dantz", [32] and in the course of a play called *Das Schauspiel teutscher Sprichwörter* [33] a song attempts graphic illustration of this *choros* (Ex. 5):

Example 5

Die Musicanten

(mit zweyer spanischen Cytharn / und einer Oberstimm oder Discant)

[32] Reprinted in Schmitz, *op. cit.*, p. 266.

[33] II, pp. 308-416. The song is on p. 401. This *Schauspiel* is a free translation of a French play, *La Comédie des Proverbes,* which Harsdörffer lists as having been published anonymously in Paris in 1633. This play, which has been ascribed to Adrien de Montluc,

Before going on to the *Tugendsterne* we may note one other appearance of a humanistic musical topic in the *Gesprächspiele*. At the beginning of the fourth volume Harsdörffer is compared, by a fellow-member of the *Fruchtbringende Gesellschaft*,[34] to a tenth Muse; he is even pictured sitting in the midst of the immortal nine,[35] and yet another strophic song commemorates his joining their company.

The poetry, pictures, and music of the *Tugendsterne*[36] present the reader a spectacle of planetary divinities transformed into, or at least blended with, a set of Christian virtues, decked out with appropriate heraldic colors, riding triumphal chariots while singing in modes suitable to their characters. The panelists of the *Gesprächspiele*, offered this entertainment by Reymund, were prepared to receive it since various elements of the spectacle had been mentioned in earlier sections of the work. The Boethian songs on the seasons gave them a sort of musical background; but besides this the panelists had gone through a *spiel* of colors, one of planets, and one on heraldic art. To give the reader equivalent preparation we must describe briefly these *spiele*. Harsdörffer's games were, he frankly admitted,[37] greatly influenced by those of late sixteenth-century

comte de Cramail, was reprinted a number of times, apparently enjoying a certain popularity; cf. H. Carrington Lancaster, *A History of French Dramatic Literature in the Seventeenth Century*, Part I, Vol. II (Baltimore, 1929), pp. 650-653. The song in the French original contains no reference to the starry dance; Harsdörffer, evidently fond of the idea, inserted this on his own.

34 For a description of this academy, founded in 1617 by Prince Ludwig of Anhalt, see Bischoff, *Harsdörffer*, ch. II, pp. 45-116.

35 This illustration is reproduced by Bischoff, *op. cit.*, p. 187.

36 In Vol. V, pp. 280-307, as *spiel* ccxiii. For the way in which the *Tugendsterne* is fitted into the fifth volume see below.

37 *FG* I, *Vorbericht*, p. Biii, where this debt is admitted; and Harsdörffer often repeats this admission.

Plate II

Italian academies, especially that of the *Intronati* in Siena. Accounts of the games played by the *Intronati*, particularly the work of Scipione Bargagli,[38] were often simply translated in the *Gesprächspiele.* The game-playing approach was cultivated by Harsdörffer (whose name in the *Fruchtbringende Gesellschaft* was "der Spielende") throughout the *Gesprächspiele*, often fused with another of his favorites, the literature of emblems.[39] The technique is simple: an emblem is shown, a tale or poem told, or the rules of a game explained; then the six speakers in turn discuss, or moralize on, the topic at hand. In the game on colors[40] the players describe the properties of the principal colors, comparing them to jewels and, for the

[38] *I Trattenimenti di Scipion Bargagli; dove da vaghe donne e da giovani Huomini rappresentati sono Honesti e dilletevoli Giuochi . . . e cantate alcune amorose canzonette . . .* (Venice, 1591). An analysis of this work is in T. F. Crane, *Italian Social Customs of the Sixteenth Century* (New Haven, 1920), pp. 297-308. Crane's book, which contains much on the Italian academies and their games, has a section on Harsdörffer and the *Gesprächspiele* (ch. XII, pp. 555-564), giving many of the sources for Harsdörffer's *spiele.* He does not mention any of the sections dealt with in this paper, however. For the *Accademia degli Intronati* see E. Cléder, *Notice sur l'academie italienne des Intronati* (Brussels, 1864), and the more recent work of Lolita Petrucci Costantini, *L'Academia degli Intronati di Siena e una sua Commedia* (Siena, 1928).

[39] Cf. L. Volkman, *Bilderschriften der Renaissance* (Leipzig, 1923), p. 109, who speaks of Harsdörffer's "etwas spielende Verknüpfung" of emblematic material. An illustration at the beginning of Vol. V of the *Gesprächspiele*, reproduced above as Pl. I, gives an idea, this one not unconnected with music, of Harsdörffer's use of emblems. In this pictorial tale the good ship German is about to founder until Fortune takes the sail, Virtue the helm, and Hope acts as anchor. With the accompaniment of Arion on the lyre (and riding his dolphin), and Orpheus on the lute (in the boat), the ship heads for shore, where the Muses, playing instruments and attended by nymphs, await it.

[40] I, pp. 83ff.

first seven colors, to the planets. Thus yellow, or gold, the color of topaz, is assigned to the sun; white or silver, the pearl, goes with the moon. Then red, the ruby, is the color of Mars; blue, the sapphire, is Jupiter's color; black, the diamond, belongs to Saturn; green, the emerald, is associated with Venus; "viol-braun" or purple, the amethyst, belongs to the changeling planet Mercury since this color is thought of as the combination of the preceding six. Harsdörffer refers in this game to a *spiel* on heraldry in the third volume of his work, and in fact the colors, stones, and planetary analogies listed here, besides having astrological signifiance, are standard parts of heraldic lore, [41] as is the comparison, made later in the *spiel,* of the seven colors with the seven ages of man.

The second volume includes a game [42] on the planets, this time associating them with metals rather than with stones or colors (Saturn = lead; Jupiter, tin; Mars, iron; Venus, copper; Mercury, quicksilver; the sun, gold; the moon, silver). Some attributes of the planets as Olympian divinities are also given: Jupiter is associated with eagles and thunder; Mercury with a snaky wand (caduceus) and with wings; the moon with water and with the quality of fickleness, etc. An astrological note is the omission of Saturn because of that leaden planet's "unglücklicher

[41] A complete statement of these analogies is contained in the heraldic manual of Sicille, herald to Alfonso V of Aragon, a 15th-century treatise which had wide circulation in its original French version and in translation. See the edition of H. Cocheris, *Le blason des couleurs en armes, livrées et devises par Sicille, Hérault d'Alphonse V, roi d'Aragon* (Paris, 1860). The planet - color - jewel - ages-of man analogies of Sicille (pp. 21-50, 57-8, 63-4) are the same as those of Harsdörffer, who in fact includes the work, in a 16th-century Italian translation, in his bibliography, although he does not refer to it in this *spiel.*

[42] II, pp. 64-66.

Wirckung".[43] The same volume has a disquisition[44] on the virtues of the number seven, with the planets in analogy to the days of the week, the days of Creation, and the ages of man. For this old neo-Platonic topic Harsdörffer uses the authority of Francesco Giorgio Veneto, whose *De Harmonia totius mundi*, first published in 1525, is one of the most exhaustive of Renaissance treatises dealing with speculative music.[45]

"Heroltskunst" is the subject of a rather long conversation in the third volume.[46] Here the planetary colors are displayed on a shield, and their use explained: in the ancient Olympic games, we are told, the contestants when engaged in combat bound these colors on their weapons to do honor to the planetary divinities.[47]

[43] The planet - metal analogies in Sicille, *op. cit.*, pp. 59ff, are not quite the same as those of Harsdörffer. The latter was using standard alchemical lore, however; cf. the identical analogies in the *Canon's Yeoman's Tale* of Chaucer *(Cant. Tales* frag. viii, ll. 826-829):

> Sol gold is, and Luna silver we threpe,
> Mars iren, Mercurie quyksilver we clepe,
> Saturnus leed, and Jupiter is tyn,
> And Venus coper, by my fader kyn!

[44] II, pp. 261-265.

[45] On Francesco Giorgi see Walker, *Spiritual Magic*, pp. 112-119; L. Thorndike, *A History of Magic and Experimental Science*, 8 vols. (New York, 1923-58), VI, p. 450f.; R. Wittkower, *Architectural Principles in the Age of Humanism* (London, 1949), p. 90f. On the number seven in music see M. Vogel, *Die Zahl Sieben in der spekulativen Musiktheorie* (Bonn, 1955), esp. pp. 43-44, where the interest of 17th-century theorists in the significance of the number seven is discussed.

[46] III, pp. 153ff.

[47] III, pp. 157-8. Cf. Sicille, *op. cit.*, pp. 63-4: "Les payens comme Alexandre, et les aultres combatans haulx princes, paravant luy et après, blasonnèrent par les sept principalles planettes, et y nommèrent leurs couleurs, et faisoyent ydolles en leurs noms qu'ilz adoroyent, et les vestoyent d'icelles couleurs, que vous voyez selon leurs noms. Et, ès batailles, chascun portoit de la couleur du Dieu

From these *spiele* the company who were to listen to Reymund sing of the *Tugendsterne* — while they looked at the engravings depicting these Planet-Virtues — learned of the planetary colors, and of at least some of the accouterments of the starry divinities. These beings are shown riding in triumphal cars over landscapes appropriate to them (see plates V-XI below). Harsdörffer's engraver [48] seems here to have been following, or rather adapting, a quite well established iconographical tradition showing the planets riding in chariots, drawn by animals associated with them, over landscapes filled with their "children", astrologically speaking. [49] A famous set of woodcuts depicting these planetary chariots, each accompanied by a short rhymed description of the planet's powers, was done in Harsdörffer's own city of Nürnberg by the sixteenth-century engraver Hans Sebald Beham. [50] Apart from minor details Harsdörffer's chariots have one

en quoy il croyoit et disoient que ce leur aydoit moult à combater". Harsdörffer's source for this tale is a 17th-century heraldic work, *Le Roy d'Armes* by M. G. de Varennes, a volume I have not been able to see; it is referred to in J. Guigard, *Bibliothèque Héraldique de la France* (Paris, 1861), p. 5.

48 I have not been able to find out who this engraver is. In some ways the illustrations in the *Gesprächspiele* are similar to the emblematic engravings of the school of Mattheus Merian (1593-1650), a school which did some work for the *Fruchtbringende Gesellschaft.* Of the illustrations in general Narciss, *op. cit.*, p. 157, says: "Die Meister Kupfer sind nach Illustrationen in anderen Büchen gestochen".

49 These planetary *trionfi* were quite common in Italy in the 15th century, spreading later to the rest of Europe. See J. Seznec, *The Survival of the Pagan Gods. The Mythological Tradition and its Place in Renaissance Humanism and Art,* transl. Barbara F. Sessions (New York: Bollingen Foundation, 1958), p. 71.

50 Beham's woodcuts, along with some Italian and German series on which they depend, are reproduced in F. Lippmann, *The Seven Planets,* transl. F. Simmonds (London, 1895), Plates E I-VII. Of Beham's series Lippmann says (pp. 12-13), "they evidently had a

consistent difference from those of Beham: the wheels of the chariots, which in Beham are filled with signs of the constellations, are marked by Harsdörffer with moral qualities, in every case two extremes between which the Virtues ride as means (see plates V-XI, and the remarks of Angelica on each of them). This change makes one think of the Platonic image of the charioteer with his good and bad horses; [51] but Harsdörffer apparently drew his concept from a source chronologically nearer, a treatise called *Solomon's Divine Arts* by the English bishop-theologian Joseph Hall (1574-1656), whose works he greatly admired. [52] The change in wheels is appropriate since Harsdörffer's chariots contain planets which are personifications of Virtues as well. His list is a quite standard combination of the three theological with the four moral virtues; however, even though most emblem books contain representations of some Virtues, this sevenfold arrangement does not seem common. [53] Nor is the exact parallel of Virtues with planets a usual one. [54] It is allowed for, even

wide circulation, and were published in a variety of editions... The numerous poor impressions extant on paper of later manufacture, show that the popularity of the series continued for many years after its first appearance".

51 See *Phaedrus, passim,* but esp. 253-254.

52 For this work and Harsdörffer's borrowing from it see below, the remarks of Reymund on the planet Venus, and note 96.

53 It does sometimes occur. In the *Emblesmes sacrez tirez de l'escriture sainté, et des peres*... par le R. P. Francois Berthod (Paris, 1665), pp. 212-267, the seven virtues are arranged in order, each having an emblem accompanied by meditations. The emblems have no planetary symbolism, however.

54 The Virtues were occasionally shown as if they were stellar divinities, as in Mantegna's *Triumph of Wisdom over Vice,* done for Isabella d'Este; cf. Seznec, *Survival of the Ancient Gods,* pp. 109, 111. The *tarocchi* sometimes ascribed to Mantegna have series of Virtues and Planets as adjoining "suits", as Seznec points out (pp.

implied, in Cornelius Agrippa,[55] but Harsdörffer's arrangement does not depend on Agrippa. His juxtaposition of planets with Virtues has nothing really unusual about it, however, and may have parallels in writers of Harsdörffer's bent.

It is not always easy to see the order in Harsdörffer's succession of *spiele;* one writer [56] has in fact described the *Gesprächspiele* as a series of topics arranged like "Kraut und Früchte" on a stand. But the *Tugendsterne* does have a definite place in the fifth volume. The *Vorrede* of the volume explains that it could be subtitled "Die Ausbildung", [57] a program of education in the three "Sinnkünsten" — painting, music, and poetry — which correspond with the mental faculties of imagination, memory, and judgment. The conversations and games of the fifth book do furnish a sort of curriculum of these arts and disciplines. Music is given a utilitarian role as an aid in memory training; when he moved away from Pythagorean notions of harmony Harsdörffer apparently thought of music in a rather prosy way, making it the servant of words and also of pictures, a complementary art rather

137-8). Seznec lists other appearances of the Virtues *near* the planets (as in the church of S. Francesco at Rimini); but a one-to-one-identity of planets and Virtues is not mentioned by him. Nor do the sixteenth-century mythographers, such as Giraldi, Natale Conti, and Cartari, mention such an exact correspondence.

[55] Cf. *Occ. phil.* III, 38; vol. II, pp. 165-168 Gaboriau, where a long list of virtues depending on the planets is given. In his encomium of the number four (II, 7; vol. I, pp. 232-238) Agrippa lists the four moral virtues under four planetary conjunctions, and in the section on the number seven (II, 10; vol. I, pp. 245-257) the seven planets are compared with everything the author can think of; no seven virtues are listed, but they could easily be supplied.

[56] Tittmann, *Die Nürnberger Dichterschule,* p. 18.

[57] V, p. Aiv.

than a self-sufficient one.[58] This helps to explain Staden's insistence, in all the music of the *Gesprächspiele,* on the simple strophic song to the exclusion of any more elaborate musical style. Speaking through the person of Reymund, Staden says, at the conclusion of the *Tugendsterne,*[60]

> I have therefore set the verses strophically, so that the music can be the more easily memorized and all sung clearly and audibly after the Italian fashion; yet the verses could also have been set in the style of the motet.

In the discussion of painting, that art as a universal language is held to be close to music, but the sense of sight is superior to the other senses because it can be exercised across great distances — in fact, the "Ehrensitz" of sight is said to be in the stars.[61] The "Dichtkunst" discussion, covering the third of the "Sinnkünsten", precedes music in the volume; it begins with a poem addressed to the same nymph Echo who is to give the prologue of the *Tugendsterne.*[62]

The bulk of the fifth volume is devoted to "Vernunftkunst" (part of another trio consisting of Grammar, Logic,

[58] Cf. I, p. 48, a discussion of "Gedächtnisskunst" in which a rhymed couplet is to be committed to memory through use of solmization syllables (placed on a musical staff) wherever the syllables *ut, re, mi,* etc., occur. This sort of thing led Krapp, *Die ästhetischen Tendenzen Harsdörffers,* p. 69, to refer to the role of music in the *Gesprächspiele* as a "blosser Stimmung".

[59] Staden's songs, whose similarity to those of Heinrich Albert has been noted (see R. Haas, *Die Musik des Barocks,* Wildpark-Potsdam, 1928, p. 172), may be said to represent a translation of Italian operatic style as Harsdörffer's *spiele* are the German equivalent of Italian *giuochi.* This paper is not concerned with Staden's style as such, but the reader will notice that the *Tugendsterne* songs though simple are not devoid of musical interest and charm.

[60] V, p. 306.

[61] V, p. 6.

[62] See below, note 86.

and Rhetoric), illustrated principally by the presentation, in translation, of an English academic comedy, *The Sophister,* with a cast made up entirely of mental categories, virtues and vices. The Oxford jurist Richard Zouche may have written this curious play, which was printed anonymously in London in 1639. Its didactic scheme and moralizing verses suited Harsdörffer so well that he has Reymund call it the best "Freudenspiele" he has read, despite the fact that it was perfomed but once, before the king at Oxford. [63] Harsdörffer's translation is a free one, but he retains the general outlines of the play. In it Discourse, a kingly hero, is sickened, even maddened, by his evil bastard son Fallacy, whose machinations are fortunately countered by the remedies of the noble Analysis. Two remedies are applied: bleeding, a medical treatment which allows Analysis to discourse on the four humors; and music. The good servant Invention is told that

> You shall doe well, if against his waking you provide some show,
> And Musick, which may welcome home his wand'ring senses. [64]

[63] *The Sophister. A Comedy.* London, 1639. Narciss, *op. cit.,* p. 8, points out that the date of the play does not correspond with Harsdörffer's English visit, or with any known visit of Charles I to Oxford. *The Sophister* is, however, a later version of a manuscript play called *Fallacy, or the Troubles of the Great Hermenia* (Br. Mus. Harl. 6869, No. 2) dated 1631, closer to the time of Harsdörffer's travel years and to a royal visit to Oxford. Cf. A. Harbage, *Cavalier Drama* (New York, 1936), p. 147n. Harsdörffer was so fond of *The Sophister* that he also made a Latin translation of it, which he published in 1647, signing himself a member of the [Neapolitan] academy of the *Otiosi.* See Narciss, *op. cit.,* p. 196.

[64] *The Sophister,* V, 1. Cf. *The Merchant of Venice,* V, i, ll. 66-68:
Come ho, and wake Diana with a hymn!
With sweetest touches pierce your mistress' ear
And draw her home with music

The music comes, "attended with a Maske", and saves the day. In *The Sophister* there is no masque, but Harsdörffer provides one: the *Tugendsterne.* Its performance comes after the play has been read, but it is clearly meant to belong within the framework of the comedy.

Although Harsdörffer does not say he saw any English masques, he does speak [65] of a French ballet performed at the court of Louis XIII, a piece including depiction of the seasons, the elements, and the planets. This description could apply to several French court ballets of the time, performances I have already spoken of. [66] The *Tugendsterne* is not a ballet, however; dancing is not even mentioned, [67] and at most a series of *tableaux vivants,* each accompanied by a strophic song, the whole linked together with instrumental symphonies, was envisaged. As the reader will see, the panelists speculated about possible performances but did not actually carry one out.

As a bit of musical humanism the *Tugendsterne* is interesting in its use of modes which correspond in their *ethos* to the characteristics of the planets. For this correspondence Harsdörffer names Glareanus [68] as his source; this is rather surprising since most of the sources cited in the *Gesprächspiele* were of more recent date than the 100-year-old *Dodecachordon.* One would have expected Harsdörffer to name Calvisius, or perhaps Mersenne, rather than Glareanus. For that matter there is no indication that Harsdörffer read Glareanus very closely; [69] if he had

[65] *Fg* II, p. 301.

[66] See above, p. 3, and note 11.

[67] Narciss, *op. cit.,* p. 95, remarks that the *Tugendsterne* "neigen stark zum Ballett"; but he does not notice the connection with *The Sophister,* nor does he give any reason for his statement.

[68] V, p. 281. See below, p. 29.

[69] The *Dodecachordon* is not even mentioned in Harsdörffer's rather large bibliography of his sources (see above, p. 5, and note 16).

he would have noticed that the great Swiss theorist for all his preoccupation with the modes never makes an explicit comparison of planets with modes, but chooses instead the more classical analogy of planets, Muses, and lyrestrings, the whole system included inside an octave of the Aeolian mode transposed to D. [70] Comparisons of modes with planets had been made by classical writers, of course, [71] and were taken up with renewed enthusiasm in the Renaissance. A well-known woodcut which appears as the frontispiece to the *Practica Musica* of Gafurius and again in his *De Harmonia Musicorum Instrumentorum,* [72] where it is given a fairly full explanation, shows a typical ordering of lyre-strings, Muses, planets, and modes. What is not so well known is that Gafurius takes his analogy — of course without acknowledgment — from his arch-rival Ramis de Pareia, in whose *Musica Practica* it appears accompanied by a simpler diagram. [73] Ramis in turn used the order of Muses found in Martianus Capella, simply adding the modes in their customary mediaeval arrangement. Glareanus, who knew the *De Harmonia* of Gafurius, [74] chose to ignore the planet-mode analogy of the older theorist; even his ordering of Muses (that of Hesiod and Herodotus) is not the same.

[70] *Dodecachordon* (Basel, 1547), pp. 99-100, with a diagram on p. 100. The scale is a descending one from the firmament to the moon.

[71] Pliny and Martianus Capella link Saturn with Dorian, Jupiter with Phrygian. The 6th-century A. D. Johannes Lydus adds a Lydian-Mars analogy; however, no complete comparison of this kind exists among ancient writers, to my knowledge.

[72] On f. lxxxir. This woodcut has been reproduced by Seznec, Warburg, and others; it may now be seen in B. C. Cannon, A. Johnson, and W. G. Waite, *The Art of Music* (New Haven: Yale University Press, 1960), p. 144.

[73] On p. 61 of J. Wolf's edition (Leipzig, 1901) of the *Musica practica.*

[74] See *Dod.* I, xxi, pp. 59-60, where the *De Harmonia* is discussed (in not very flattering terms).

To return to Harsdörffer: if he did read Glareanus rather than get his information second hand (since his description of the *ethos* of the modes seems to be in each case a simplification of Glareanus' comments [75] it is rather hard to decide this point), he simply substituted the modes, which if becoming archaic were still known to his prospective readers, for the Greek-lyre-string names, for which German equivalents would have been clumsy and hard to explain. Harsdörffer's arrangement of the modes (D, E, A, G, F, C, B♭) and planets (sun, moon, Venus, Mars, Jupiter, Mercury, Saturn) is also unorthodox, both musically and astronomically, so much so that in the appendix to Vol. V, where the music is printed, the reader is advised that "The order is done according to the Virtues and not according to the planets or modes". [76] This rearrangement seems at first sight a trivial change, but to a fifteenth- or sixteenth-century scholar versed in neo-Platonic cosmology it would have seemed horrendous, a wilful disruption of the universal order. The list of planet — lyre-string — virtue correspondences in such a late sixteenth-century work as the *Galliade* of Le Fèvre de la Boderie, for example, makes the virtues conform to the normal (Ptolemaic) order of planets. [77] But for Harsdörffer neo-Platonic astrology was just another *spiel,* one whose rules could easily be changed if they seemed to conflict with something as im-

[75] See below, Harsdörffer's descriptions of individual modes, and the notes giving Glareanus' descriptions. The latter does not always give very clear-cut characterizations of the modes, and this may account for some seeming discrepancies between the simplified statements in the *Tugendsterne* and the more scholarly descriptions of the *Dodecachordon.*

[76] V, p. Mmii. The introduction to the musical appendix (written by Staden himself?) is given in translation below, note 85.

[77] *La Galliade, ou de la Revolution des Arts et sciences* (Paris, 1578), f. 88r-91r.

portant as Christian virtues. Through all the humanistic trappings of his writings Harsdörffer lets show his most characteristic quality — described by one writer as "der deutscher Ernst". [78] And just such a detail as the rearrangement of the classical order of planets and modes shows that the musical cosmology of the ancient world no longer had any real meaning in the seventeenth century. As for the music of the *Tugendsterne*, Staden's efforts are innocent of humanistic strivings; the modal *ethos* in his songs would perhaps have surprised Glareanus just as much as it would any Greek theorist. But the very ingenuousness with which classical precepts about modes are mixed with midseventeenth-century figured-bass tonality gives Staden's music charm and, in its modest way, integrity of style, a quality the learned Harsdörffer somehow sought in vain.

[78] See Tittman, *op. cit.*, p. 5.

Die Tugendsterne

DIE TUGENDSTERNE

Reymund: As I thought over the comedy just now presented,[79] it occurred to me that Tacitus attempted to put to use on the isle of Lesbos almost the same political arts that Fallacy[80] here employs, as the copious account of Trajano Boccalini tells us.[81] But Tacitus had just as little success with his political sophistry, having to escape in disguise to Parnassus, and having to admit that Heaven and Earth are not so far apart, snow and coal not so unlike in color as paper instructions on the art of government are distant from its actual working out — or that a regime which is not based on virtue and honesty cannot in the long run remain calm and at peace. For this reason I have decided to set forth a pageant of the seven Virtues, which are, by way of analogy, the seven planets. Through these, blessed influences are poured forth upon governments. Since, moreover, Glareanus compares the seven voices or modes[82] of music

[79] *The Sophister.* See above, p. 22, and note 63.

[80] One of the principal characters in *The Sophister,* in fact the Sophist himself; *Trügewicht* in the German version of the play.

[81] The story is in Boccalini's *Ragguagli di Parsano e Pietra del Paragone Politico,* Centura Prima, Ragguaglio xxix (not xvii, as Harsdörffer says in a marginal note), vol. I, pp. 89-94 in the edition of G. Rua and L. Firpo, 3 vols. (Bari, 1910-12, 1948). Reymund's sentence about heaven and earth, snow and coal, is a paraphrase of Tacitus' account, made to Pliny the Younger, of his failure on Lesbos.

[82] "Stimmen oder Töne", the *voces* and *modi* of Glareanus.

with the seven planets and their properties, [83] I shall use this comparison in my exposition of the Virtues. Whatever may be missing in my representation of this pageant I leave to the present company to supply.

Vespasian: The gentleman will now deal with music as the third of the sensuous arts. [84]

Rey.: Before I begin to do so I should like you all to observe how the Most High Creator of mankind has bound up whatever is necessary to human life with a quite particular pleasure, — as in eating, drinking, sleeping, and the propagation of the species — thereby lightening and sweetening our toilsome life.

Degenwert: Music must have been invented soon after the Creation of the World, just for such an end, such innocent enjoyment.

Julia: Another blameless use of music is the awakening of greater piety at the holy service.

Rey.: Indeed it is from God Himself — proper and almost necessary for warfare, for driving out evil spirits and thoughts, for celebrating Holy Communion, and for every kind of blameless pastime.

Angelica: The pageant promised by the gentleman is long in getting started.

Rey: I haven't yet quite tuned my lute.

Cassandra: A lot of tuning, but not much playing ("Viel Stimmens, wenig Schlagens").

Vesp: I recall that Pythagoras, as it were bewitched by

[83] Cf. *Dodecachordon* II, xii, p. 94, where Glareanus says that such a comparison is made by others. In II, xiii, p. 99, Glareanus interprets a famous passage from the *Somnium Scipionis* of Cicero to equate the eight spheres with the seven intervals in the octave and hence with the seven octave-species. This is as close as he comes to the planet-mode analogy; see above, p. 24.

[84] See above, p. 20.

Tenor oder Discant.
Still
Höret mich Tochter der Grüfften (in Lüfften) erschallen! höret bewe-
Still
de Flammen fügen/und schmiegen den Himmel und Erden zusammen.

Echo der Verredner.
Still
gen(und regen)der Gegenstimm hallen! sehet von ferne (der Sterñe) hochglänzẽ-
Still
priefet(wie triefet) von oben der Wolken Gerüchte / schauet/ wie schossen und
Mm iij
sprossen

Plate III

his studies of numbers, said that he heard the lovely music given off by the starry motions. We here await with longing the music which the Planet-Virtues are really going to bring to our ears. [85]

* * * *

[85] The poetry of the *Tugendsterne* is printed opposite the illustrations; the music [see Pl. II above for its appearance] is given in an appendix at the end of the volume, with a title page and preface of its own, thus:

The VII { Virtues
Planets
Modes or Tones } Pageant

Set to elegant melodies by Sigmund Gottlieb Staden.

PREFACE.

Although a complete account of this pageant may be seen under the same title in the 13th conversation-game, still it was thought necessary to remind the reader that the seven modes in music have a precise relationship with the powers attributed to the planets, and that in the knowledge of these seven modes consists all of music — about which one can read further in Glareanus.

In the symphonies or intonations the individual parts of the small format are not completely worked out but can be completed; just as the poetry, paintings, and other instructions in the conversation-game are far from final completeness, and are left to all lovers of German for help toward finished state.

Echo or Repeated Sound is the opening speaker.

[There follows a list of planets, modes with their key-letters, modal properties, and Virtues.]

It should be noted that the bass part is to be played each time on the "Instrument" [in another place, quoted by Schmitz, *op. cit.*, p. 266, "Instrument" is defined as "theorbe theorbata", but Harsdörffer says that one could instead use "Geigenwerk / eine Lauten / eine Positiv", as long as the singers can be heard]; and the ordering is done according to the Virtues, not the planets or tones. The rest is self-explanatory.

* * * *

It is to be hoped that the music is self-explanatory; but one additional remark may be made here. The "Reimmaass" given before

The speaker of the preamble is Echo, [86] who, hovering in the air at the mouth of a rocky cavern, sings these double-rhymed lines: [87]

Hear me, the daughter of caves, in air sound forth!
O hear the tones of echoes move and rise up;
See, from afar, the bright-shining flames of the stars
Blend and entwine the heavens and earth together!
O praise how the rainclouds pour down from on high!
Regard, how ripening buds grow and spring forth;
Golden beams color the teeming fields;
Quickening, mountains, hills, fields and forests glow.
Suchlike ornament adorns the gifts of the Virtues,
Which have powers just as mighty and active
[as stars].
The planet-Virtues rule men in their needs;
Mighty and splendid, the heavenly orders the earthly.
Thus the stars sing forth, and lead the heavenly dance

each modal song is indicative of Harsdörffer's interest in prosody, and of Staden's close following of this prosody in the music, which is actually a sort of German *musique mesurée*. The "Reimmaass" indications are not always precise, but they are given here as in the original, with the 'enlightened' reader [cf. note 88 below] encouraged to correct them; the prosodic scheme for Saturn-Temperance is so corrupt, however, that I have corrected it.

86 Echo is a nymph beloved by Harsdörffer; in the section of Vol. V called "Die Dichtkunst" there is an amusing poem adressed to her, full of the droll internal rhymes used in the preamble to the *Tugendsterne* (for instance, Echo's beauty is said to be "wie Narcissus in dem Bach", to which the nymph answers, "Ach."). Cf. also the beginning of *Seelewig* in Vol. IV, where "Frau Musica" is praised by the conversationalists, and is said to be "auf Erden der Echo oder Widerhall der himmlischen Freuden". The chorus of nymphs at the end of Act II of *Seelewig* uses the same device as do those examples just quoted.

87 For the internal rhymes, not reproduced in the translation but essential for the echo effect, see the German text printed with the music.

Which wins over men's senses and wondrously
thrives.[88]

* * * *

Jul.: I understand by the just-finished preface that as the planets rule the greater world, so the seven Arch-Virtues rule the lesser one.

Vesp.: Whoever sees a misstuning is looking at a godless and depraved man, and will find that feelings of regret and distaste rise up in him. For our spirits are created in a kind of musical way by Nature,[89] so that everything which exceeds proper measure must seem wrong to us. Thus do we note that the injustice some beggar does a boy, or the unseemliness in the new ways of dressing, or the anger of a man towards his innocent servant, etc., all trouble us even if they do not apply directly to us.

Ang.: Thus it follows that as the happy influence of the stars makes the earth flower, so the Virtues make men happy.

Deg.: Since Echo has her home in the air, as it were between heaven and earth, this nymph is with right the speaker of the preamble; yet in her place one could have introduced the Milky Way,[90] or Jacob's ladder.

88 In this poem and indeed in all that follow there are a great many discrepancies — too many to list here — between the text as given in the body of the book and as printed with the music in the appendix. Harsdörffer knew that his work was full of errors, but he was quite unconcerned about it; hoping that "die Druckfehler wird der Vernünfftige Leser leichtlich entschuldigen" (V, *Vorrede,* p. B), he explains that the printers are not used to work of this kind, and that the author has no time for proofreading!

89 The "musical" nature of man is a favorite theme of Vespasian, who mentions this concept of *musica humana* several times; cf. p. 11 above.

90 This may be a reference to the Milky Way as the abode of blessed spirits after death, a neo-Pythagorean notion developed by Macrobius; see the *Comm. in Somn. Scip.* II, iii, p. 593 Eyssenhardt.

Cass.: If one wanted to perform this pageant without spending much money, one could depict all the personages by painting them on the tapestry which, according to scenic art, would decorate the stage at the very back. Then the voices, accompanied by lute or theorboe, could be heard behind the curtain.

Rey.: Now comes the first person of the pageant, Faith; her star is the sun, her tone or mode D, her song the following:

1.

Darkened hearts, sleeping senses,
  Now waken! awaken! arouse yourselves;
Look at the crimson-glowing spot
  Which even now in your souls
The heavenly sun stirs up
  Through joy of believing.

2.

As the beaming taper of heaven dawns,
  The earth comes to flower, the fields are adorned;
So the soul is nourished, the world enlightened
  By godly light, which fires in the heart,
And lets itself be seen,
  Its trusting Faith.

3.

The earth would lie dark,
  Grow savage, waste, sink into dust,
If its daily life-giving round of fruitful beams
  The sun, as it were changing horses, should omit;
So must men's souls,
  Without Faith, be tormented.

Jul.: In this song Faith is compared to the sun.

Vesp.: The planets should be clothed in heraldic colors, [91] and indeed the sun should be fire-colored, or in a golden cloth (the word costs nothing) edged by flame; in the way that one for that matter usually depicts Faith.

Ang.: Now I recall that Herr Reymund mentioned earlier [92] that pagan pictures can be used and written on in Christian fashion. In this connection I should add that in my opinion the sun, or Faith, sits on a noble triumphal chariot, the two wheels of which might be named Unbelief and Superstition.

Deg.: The mode D, otherwise called Dorian, is splendid and majestic. [93] The landscape might be of churches and vineyards.

Vesp.: The animals drawing the sun's chariot could be lions, since the sun is at its hottest in the constellation of Leo, and this beast is, besides, the strongest and most admirable of animals.

Rey.: Since this planet-Virtue has now been portrayed, there follows Hope, whose star is the moon, and whose tone or mode is E. The song can be this one, or one even better fashioned:

1.

The moon rules over the silver sea,
  Rolling it over the parched sands,
Showing the salt-dry land of the coast,
  And leading the high-riding army of waves;
The violent eddies tremble in time
  With swollen floods,
And build out of water mountain, hill, and vale.

[91] Cf. p. 16, above.

[92] In the *Vorrede* of Vol. V.

[93] Cf. *Dod.* II, xxi, p. 118: "Dorius contra Maiestatem quandam ac gravitatem praese fert, quam admirari facilius sit, quem explicare".

2.

So rages and storms the tyrant of hell,
  As peoples and lands are drowned in deceits;
Yet Hope fast anchors all believers,
  Who ride far above the waves of misfortune.
Hope, for the godly, assures the heart.
  If there should approach
Deadly pain and the ragings of hell.

3.

The silvery coin, it gleams, reflected;
  It fights and conquers, rules and directs;
Valleys it lowers, mountains are cleft,
  It moulds and fashions the chains of the world.
O fatal thoughts! the band of believers,
  Can more surely let drop
The anchor of Hope on the eternal strand.

* * * *

Jul.: I take the meaning of this song to be that as the moon rules over the sea and as gold rules the world, so Hope governs the pious.

Vesp.: This planet-Virtue might be clothed in white or silver.

Ang.: The wheels of the chariot are Mistrust and Despair.

Deg.: The mode is E, called Phrygian, sad and melancholy; [94] the painted backdrop, rocks and the sea.

Cass.: The animals pulling the chariot might be sea-horses, as were in other times depicted with Neptune.

Rey.: Although one doesn't find such horses in the sea now, there were formerly curious monsters and wonders

[94] Cf. *Dod.* II, xxiii, p. 123: "[Phrygius] habeat nescio quid lachrymabile et quod animos ad fletum exciter . . ."

there — yet one should not take the painters and poets literally in this respect. Now, after Hope follows Love: the star is Venus, the tone or mode A:

1.

Whoever beholds my charming, lovely face,
Regards these coral-red, laughing lips,
Sees next, over tender uncovered breast
Gold-gleaming hair, gently moving with desire,
Choose not, out of hotly impious lusting,
Voluptuous love.

2.

The pure flames of my heartfelt, pious desires
Unite all men with heavenly joys;
Enlist on earth the undying favor of the Most High,
Gleam and glow steadily with wondrous fervor.
Look how souls inspired by godly desires
Burn with love.

3.

Shall rocks and caves take echoes in air,
Fire come from spark, and flame from flame enkindle?
So it is when, from heavenly grace, there begins
Love of neighbor, from Faith with patient Hope;
It brings out of modest, good-hearted desire,
The fruits of Love.

* * * *

Jul.: In this pageant the distinction between love of God, love of neighbor, and sinful wanton love is made clear.

Vesp.: According to heraldic art this planet-Virtue must be dressed in green.

Ang.: Love is depicted with little children because the fervor of a mother's love can be compared only with itself. One chariot wheel is Hate, the other Uncontrolled Love.

Deg.: The mode is A, called Aeolian, charming and graceful, [95] the painted scene of harvest-time.

Cass.: The two animals with the triumphal chariot are doves. These three Virtues may indeed travel in the clouds since they are particularly spiritual and directed towards God; even love of one's neighbor can be understood as a counterpart, echo, or flame springing from that Divine love.

Rey.: Samuel Hahl [sic], a famous Englishman, has made up a complete manual of virtues or ethics from the writings of the wise king Solomon. It is a fine little book, well worth reading, and will soon be translated into our language and be printed. [96] Since, however, we are not in the habit of adorning ourselves with foreign feathers, we must continue, and portray the remaining Virtues.

[95] *Dod.* II, xvii, pp. 104-105: "[Aeolius] . . . jucunda, ac supra modum dulci suavitate gratam habet severitatem . . ."

[96] The work to which Harsdörffer refers is probably *Solomon's Divine Arts,* particularly its first section, "Ethics or morals". This paraphrase of Proverbs and Ecclesiastes is not by "Samuel Hahl" but by Joseph Hall (1574-1656), bishop of Exeter. The text may be found in Vol. VIII, pp. 222-227 of Hall's *Works,* ed. P. Wynter, 10 vols. (Oxford, 1863). In the book on ethics Hall gives the four virtues of Prudence, Justice, Temperance, and Fortitude as requisite for human felicity. Defining virtue as the mean between extremes, Hall sometimes gives two extremes between which a virtue lies; thus Prudence has "Overwise" and "Foolish" as extremes. Harsdörffer's "Räder" are clearly influenced by Hall, as the wheels of Mercury-Prudence's chariot ("überwitz" and "Unverstand") show. Whether the German translation promised by Harsdörffer ever materialized I cannot say.

Strength, or magnanimity, exemplified in the planet Mars, is executed in the G mode, with these words:

1.

The god of war, he washes his strong fist in blood;
He rages through the world with sharp and polished sword,
Leaving land and folk in pain and fiery passion
To bid defiance to his never-softened heart, his mischief.

2.

I know my strength to lie in hope and patience,
Shunning the broad and sinful path of vice.
Or if my guilt should burden me, upon this path,
With heavy punishment for sin, I'll suffer willingly.

3. [not given with the music]

Or even if the anger of the Lord should crush my soul,
Break all my bones with fearful birthpangs,
As if He wished, full of rage, to thrust me into hell,
Yet in His solace shall my heart and hand remain.

4.

Christlike valor and strong hero's courage
Let one earn through death the martyr's crown.
When the band of tyrants persecutes with fire and water
As Christian knight one dies with joyful trust.

* * * *

Jul.: Courage and magnanimity consist not in the armed might of soldiers but in persevering patience at times of temptation. Job showed this virtue when he said, "Though thou slayest me, O Lord, yet will I trust in Thee". [97] This one can see expressly in the third commandment.

[97] Job 13:15.

Vesp.: With the words "When the band of tyrants persecutes with fire and water" Herr Reymund doubtless was thinking of some martyrs who were tortured not only with fiery implements but also in winter in the coldest water. The heraldic color for this planet-Virtue is red.

Ang.: This planet should be depicted as men formerly showed Strength, with two pillars. The chariot wheels are Faint-heartedness and Rashness.

Deg.: The mode is G, *mixto Lydius,* ardent and stimulating to fight. [98]

Cass.: The animals on the chariot are stags, which Nature arms with horns.

Rey.: The fifth pageant brings on Justice, [99] or Jupiter, with little Anacreontic verses set in the F mode.

1.

The arrogant blasphemer
  Has, in time of war,
Through robbery and plunder,
  Made justice all forgotten;
Forgotten and laid low;
  Laid low and all but silenced.
Yet I have not discarded
  The pious men of God,
Who struggle with the wicked,
  And mix their bread with tears.

[98] *Dod.* II, xxvi, pp. 133-135, the chapter on the Mixolydian mode, gives no clear *ethos* for this mode, there being too many conflicting accounts about it in classical writers.

[99] In the list of errors at the back of Vol. V it is stated that Justice "mit verbundenen Augen sollen gebildet seyn".

2.

Just as my visage blinds,
  Blinds so not to spare,
To spare that person
  Who turns away from God;
So shall the scales be righted,
  And sword's point shall destroy
Defilers of their conscience;
  To settle sinners' debts,
To crown all pious works —
  For this I am sent.

3.

If for the crowd of poor men
  The law should here do nothing,
And, driven back to fight,
  They later, parched, gasp;
There yet is hope for them,
  The judgment seat of God.
Oh! when they struggle here,
  And call for help from Him,
God easily can free them,
  His justice is not sold.

Jul.: The justice of the children of God consists in our Savior's words: "Do unto others as you would have them do unto you". Indeed what we render to our neighbors God will render to us.

Vesp.: The herald's color of this planet is blue.

Ang.: The backdrop is described in the song. The wheels are Indulgence and Cruelty.

Deg.: The mode is F, called Lydian, somewhat melancholy [100] to listen to.

Cass.: Two eagles pull the chariot.

Rey.: Now comes Wisdom or Prudence, whose planet is Mercury, whose song is trochaic, in the C mode:

1.

While man, the weakling, fumbles
  In the deep and mournful vale,
He shall not altogether live
  As solitary as the beasts.
Prudent wit and understanding
  Are the staff he takes in hand,
Which lights, which leads,
  On every path and road.

2.

This mirror shows, as do these snakes,
  That almost nothing can succeed
Which has not first been thought out well
  And with sagacity begun.
This animal all blue and gold
  Teaches wisdom's graceful mien
In comings, in goings
  On every path and road.

[100] *Dod.* II, xxv, pp. 127-128. As in the case of Mixolydian, so for the Lydian mode Glareanus gives a number of conflicting views. Plato's opinion of it and its subforms as "lugubres sive querulas" (from the *Republic),* which Harsdörffer seems to adapt, is quoted by Glareanus, but he actually thinks Lydian to be an "egregium Modum" because it was so much used by the writers of Gregorian chants.

3

More, this wisdom shall produce
Modest, proper, candid thought
(Shown here by the pair of swans),
  Ruling all the acts of men.
We shall not, all blindly faring,
  In the devil's hellish circle
Often blunder, often fall,
  On every path and road.

* * * *

Jul.: The content of this song is easy: man should be in every act as wise as serpents and as unspotted as swans, whose feathers remain white even in the midst of mud and filth.

Vesp.: Mercury is god of the arts; he carries a serpent-wand, and can well be connected with this virtue of Wisdom. The heraldic color is purple.

Ang.: The wheels are Corrupt or Excessive Wit and Lack of Understanding.

Deg.: The mode is C, Ionian, gay and pretty. [101]

Cass.: The animals on the chariot have been spoken of.

Rey.: The last pageant is that of Temperance; the remaining planet is Saturn, the mode ♮ or *b dur;* the poem consists of long trochaic verses, thus:

1.

Although I am indeed the last of all the sister Virtues,
Their beauty cannot be complete unless I lend my aid.
They present the spirit's gifts with ne'er too well-praised charm,

[101] *Dod.* II, xxi, p. 118: "[Ionicus] in totum saltationibus addictus, suavitatis ac iucunditatis multum habet, severitatis prope nihil". A similar statement may be found in II, xx, p. 115.

I bring them strength of frame through measure, limit, time.

This quickly aging life
Can give us no pleasure
Unless measure and propriety
With healthy body are enjoyed.

2.

Human heart and head, they cherish sweet and bitter joys,
And, the awaited time come, seldom enjoy a happy day;
If they have great strength, they glut on flesh and wine
Till sated, sickened; then come sinful fleshly acts.

For if our body is exhausted
And coupled with weakness,
Soon the spirit also dies —
That which is Virtue's workshop.

3.

The man who in his walk of life stays on the middle course,
And can be temperate in eating, drinking, sleeping, waking, love,
Will live out his appointed days in health, free from vexation,
E'en when he sometimes starves or floats in sought-for excess.

Thus it is in our hands
To stave off from us things unpleasant;
For he who loves not Temperance
Troubles no one more than himself.

* * * *

Jul.: Temperance here boasts that no other Virtue can very well exist without her; temperance keeps men healthy and prevents all evils. Whence it is said: 'The mouth is man's doctor and his executioner'.

Vesp.: The proverb that 'man can bear anything except good fortune' is à propos here. The heraldic color is black.

Ang.: The wheels of Temperance's chariot are on one side Satiety, on the other side deliberate Starvation.

Deg.: The mode is called *Spurius*, or the cast-off ♮.[102]

Cass.: The animals drawing the chariot are two tigers.

Rey: Now the whole pageant has been set forth. In an actual performance there would be much more to observe, depending on the actors one wished to employ, and the money one wished to spend. I have set the verses strophically so that one could easily learn the music by heart and be able to sing it all clearly and distinctly after the Italian fashion; however, the poetry could have been set in the style of the motet. Between each of the planet-Virtues a symphony or artistic intonation-

[102] Staden has to this point conformed, despite the generally tonal cast of his dance-like continuo songs, to the intervallic content of the ecclesiastical modes; now, the six authentic modes having already been used, he has to face the problem of selecting arbitrarily one of the "hypo" or "hyper" modes. Hyperaeolian is a rather strange choice. Glareanus (II, xviii, p. 112) terms this a "rejecto modo" and will have nothing to do with it because of the tritone it involves. Only 'moderns' in search of novelty employ it, he adds. Glareanus points out that if one alters the first or fifth degree to rid oneself of the tritone, the result is a transposition of Lydian or Phrygian. Staden may have acted on this hint; he solves the tritone problem quite simply by using a signature of one flat, by alternating cadences on Bb, F, and D, and by using Eb wherever the tritone threatens. This actually results in a transposition of the Lydian mode, but the conversationalists, who are not really concerned with the finer points of music theory, let it pass.

piece [103] must be executed so that the whole work may be unified.

Jul.: If velvet, satin, and damask could be used for clothing, and the whole performance played at night with lamps, it would all be more effective.

Vesp.: Herr Reymund has indeed formed his poetry in accordance with the properties of each mode; he deserves praise and thanks from all understanding lovers of art for this quite new invention.

[103] "... eine Symphonie oder künstliche Anstimmung des Tons ..."; Harsdörffer's reluctance to use foreign words extends even to musical terms, so he adds this cumbersome German equivalent for *sinfonia.* The function of these instrumental interludes is, of course, to set the modal *ethos* for the songs which follow each of them.

Plate IV

Echo der Vorredner

Das Reymmass —◡◡/—◡◡/—◡◡/—◡

Symphonia vor dem I. Aufzuge

Mit 3 Corneten oder Zinken, und einem Positiv

Plate V

Das Reimmaass des folgenden I. Aufzugs — — ∪ ∪ — ∪ — ∪ ∪ — ∪ / — — ∪ ∪ — ∪ — ∪ ∪ — /
— — ∪ ∪ — ∪ — ∪ ∪ — / — — ∪ ∪ — ∪ — ∪ ∪ — ∪ /
— — ∪ ∪ — ∪ — — ∪ ∪ —

Der I. Aufzug. Der Glaub ⊙ D. Dorius

Symphonie zu den zweyten Aufzug

Mit 3 Discant-Violen und einem Instrument

Plate VI

Das Reimmaass des II. Aufzugs — — ◡◡ — ◡◡ — ◡◡ — / — — ◡◡ — ◡◡ — ◡◡ — ◡ /
— — ◡◡ — ◡◡ — ◡◡ — ◡ / — — ◡◡ — ◡◡ — ◡◡ — /
— — ◡◡ — ◡ / — — ◡◡ — / — ◡◡ — ◡ /
— — ◡◡ — ◡◡ — ◡◡ — /

Der II. Aufzug. Die Hoffnung ☽ E. Phrygius

* The notes in the treble give this 3/8 bar; the bass has a semibreve. If the latter is correct the bar should perhaps be an ordinary 2/4 one, with the a and b of the treble read as eighth-notes.

Symphonia zu dem III. Aufzug

Mit Diskantgeigen und einer Theorbe

Note: The remainder of the German text for Aufzüge II through VII will be found at the end of the volume.

Plate VII

—◡◡—◡◡—◡◡—◡◡—◡ / —◡◡—◡◡—◡◡—◡◡—◡ / —◡◡—◡◡—◡◡—◡◡— / —◡◡—◡◡—◡◡—◡◡— /
—◡◡—◡◡—◡◡—◡◡—◡ / —◡◡—◡ /

Der III. Aufzug. Die Liebe ♀ A. Aeolius

Sinfonia zu dem IV. Aufzuge

Mit zwei Clarinen und einer Posaunen

Plate VIII

Das Reimmaas. ∪—∪—∪—∪—∪—∪— / ∪—∪—∪—∪—∪—∪—∪ /
∪—∪—∪—∪—∪—∪— / ∪—∪—∪—∪—∪—∪—∪ /

Der IV.*Aufzug. Die Starke ♂ G. Mixtolydius

*The song of Mars is fourth in the text but fifth in order in the musical appendix.

Symphonie zu dem V. Aufzug

Mit 2 Flöten und einem Geigen-Instrument

Plate IX

Reimmaas ◡—◡—◡—◡ Nach der Lateiner Anacreontischen Verslein

Der V. Aufzug. Die Gerechtigkeit ♃ F. Lydius

Symphonia vor dem VI. Aufzug

Mit 2 Schalmeyen und einem Regal

Plate X

Das Reimmaas. —∪—∪—∪—∪ / —∪—∪—∪— / ∪—∪—∪—∪— /
∪—∪—∪—∪—∪ / —∪—∪—∪—— / —∪—∪—∪— / ∪∪— —∪∪—∪ / —∪∪—∪ /

Der VI. Aufzug. Die Vorsichtigkeit ☿ C. Ionicus

Symphonia vor dem VII. Aufzug

Mit 2 Zwergpfeiffen und einer Harffen

Plate XI

Reimmaas. —∪—∪—∪— / —∪—∪—∪—∪ / —∪—∪—∪— / —∪—∪—∪—∪ /
—∪—∪—∪—∪ / —∪—∪—∪— / —∪—∪—∪—∪ / —∪—∪—∪— /
—∪—∪—∪—∪ / —∪—∪—∪—∪ / —∪—∪—∪— / —∪—∪—∪— /

Der VII. Aufzug Die Mässigkeit ♄ B. Hyperaeolius

DER I. AUFZUG. DER GLAUB. D. DORIUS.

1. Verfinsterter Hertzen, schlaffende Sinne, erwachet!
strekket euch fort! erwachet!
beschauet den purpurgläntzenden Ort,
dass jetzo in eurer Seele beginne
die himmlische Sonne durch glaubige Wonne.

2. Wie taget des Himmels stralende Kertze
beblümet die Erden, schminket das Feld;
So nehret die Seel, erleuchtet die Welt,
Das göttliche Liecht, das feuret im Hertze,
und lässet sich schauen,
in Glaubens-Vertrauen.

3. Es würde die Erden finster erliegen,
verwilden, veröden, sinken zu Grund,
Wann täglich nicht dieses erschaffene Rund
der fruchtenden Sonne Stralen ümstiegen.
so müssen die Seelen
ohn Glauben sich qwelen.

DER II. AUFZUG. DIE HOFFNUNG. E. PHRYGIUS.

1. Der Monde regieret das silberne Meer,
er waltzet es von den geschrundenen Sande,
er weiset der Ufersaltz-trokkene Lande,
und führet der Wellen hochfahrendes Heer.
Die hastigen Struden erbeben zu mal,
mit schwülstigen Fluten,
und bilden aus Wasser, Berg, Hügel und Thal.

2. So wütet und tobet der Höllen Tyrann,
weil Völker und Länddder in Argen ersoffen,
doch ankert festgründig der Glaubigen Hoffen,
des Ungelükks Wellen weitwallen hintan.
Das Hoffen der Frommen versichert das Hertz
und solten herkommen
die Höllengewitter und tödlicher Schmerz.

3. Es prachtet geachtet das silberne Gelt,
es krieget und sieget, es schaltet und waltet;
versenket die Thäler und Berge zerspaltet,
es niedet und schmiedet die Fessel der Welt.
Mordsuchtiges Denken! der Glaubigen Band
kan sicherer senken
den Anker der Hoffnung am ewigen Strand.

DER III. AUFZUG. DIE LIEBE. A. AEOLIUS.

1. Welche mein Lieb-und erfreuliches Angesicht achtet,
diese Corallen-boldsüssliche Lippen betrachtet,
siehet benebens ob zartlich entdekketer Brust,
schweben goldgläntzender Haare behägliche Lust;
wähne nicht etwan aus hitzig frechbulendem Triebe;
üppische Liebe.

2. Meiner hertzbrünstigen Neigungen reinliche Flammen
fügen mit himmlischen Freuden die Menschen zusammen,
werben auf Erden des Höchsten unsterbliche Gunst,
blinkern und finkern beharrlich mit seltener Brunst.
Sehet die Seelen, aus Göttlich begeissertem Triebe,
brennen vor Liebe.

3. Felsen und Gruften, in Luften, das Gegenwort nennen,
Feuer von Funken und Flammen von Flammen
entbrennen,
solcher Gestalte beginnet von Göttlicher Huld,
Liebe des Nechsten der Glaube mit Hofnungs Gedult;
bringet aus gütig-demütigen hertzlichen Triebe
Früchte der Liebe.

DER IV. AUFZUG. DIE STARKE. G. MIXTOLYDIUS.

1. Es wäscht der Krieges Gott oft seine Händ im Blut,
und raset durch die Welt mit blankgeschärfften Eisen,
Er setzet Land und Leut in Feuerlohe Glut
sein niemals weichend Herz und frevel Trotz zu weisen.

2. Ich weise meine Stärk' in Hoffnung und Gedult,
bemüht, den Sündenweg der Laster zu vermeiden.
Ob mich auf diesem Pfad belastet meine Schuld,
mit schwerer Sündenstraf, so will ichs willig leiden.

3. Wann auch des HERREN Zorn zerknirschte meine
Seele,
zerbreche mein Gebein mit strengen Mutterweben,
als wolte er Grimmes voll mich stossen in die Höle,
sol doch auf seinem Trost mein Hertz und Mund
bestehen.

4. Der Christen Tapferkeit und fester Heldenmuht,
vermag die Marterkron durch Marter zu erwerben.
Wann der Tyrannen Rott verfolgt mit Flut und Blut,
kan man mit Freudentrost als Christi Ritter sterben.

DER V. AUFZUG. DIE GERECHTIGKEIT.

F. LYDIUS.

1. Der Freveler vermessen
hat in den Kriegeszeiten,
gemacht, durch Raub und Beuten
Gerechtigkeit vergessen,
vergessen und erliegen,
erliegen und verschmiegen;
doch bin ich nicht entsessen,
den frommen Gottesleuten,
die Sünd und Laster meiden,
und Brot mit Threnen essen.

2. Wie mein Gesicht verblendet,
verblendet nicht zu schonen,
zu schonen der Personen,
die sich von Gott gewendet:
So wird die Waage richten,
und dieses Schwert vernichten,
die ihr Gewissen schändet,
dem Sündenlaster lohnen,
der Frommen Werk bethronen;
darzu bin ich gesendet.

3. Sol auch dem armen Hauffen
das Recht hiernicht gedeyen,
und sie vergnügte entzweyen,
nach dem sie, durstig, schnauffen:
So steht doch ihrem Hoffen
des Höchsten Richtstul offen;
Ach wann sie dahin lauffen
und Gottes Hülf anschreyen,
wird er sie leicht befreyen,
sein Recht ist nicht zu kauffen.

DER VI. AUFZUG. DIE VORSICHTIGKEIT.
C. IONICUS.

1. Weil die schwachen Menschen schweben
in dem tieffen Threnen Thal,
sollen sie nicht all zu Mal,
einsam als die Wilden leben.
Vorsicht, Klugheit und Verstand
ist der Stab in ihrer Hand;
dieser begleitet und leitet
auf Wegen und Stegen.

2. Dieser Spiegel, diese Schlangen
deuten, dass fast nie geglükkt,
was nicht vorbedacht erblikkt,
und ist weisslich angefangen.
Das so gelblich, blaue Thier
lehret sie der Klugheit Zier;
zu stehen und gehen
auf Wegen und Stegen.

3. Doch, sol diese Klugheit führen
Einfalt, Zucht und Redlichkeit
(durch die Schwaanen angedeut)
und der Menschen Thun regiren.
Wollen wir nicht blinder Weiss,
in des Satans Höllenkreiss,
oftermals wallen und fallen,
auf Wegen und Stegen.

DER VII. AUFZUG. DIE MÄSSIGKEIT.
B. HYPERAEOLIUS.

1. Ob ich gleich die letzte bin an der Tugend-Schwester-
Reyen,

mag doch ihre schöne nicht, ohne mein Behuf gedeyen;
führen sie die Seelen gaben mit nie statt belobter Zier;
so bring ich die liebes Kräfften ihnen nur zu Dienst
herfür.
Dieses kurz betagte Leben,
kan uns keine Wonne geben
wann nicht Zucht und Mässigkeit,
mit gesundem Leib erfreut.

2. Aller Menschen Herz und Sinn bitter-süsse Wollust
gehet,
und doch in erwünschtem Stand selten gute Tag
erträget,
haben sie verlangte Stärke, so verreitzt sie Fleisch
und Blut,
zu bekränkter Leibesfülle, nechst der Buhler
Sündenglut.
Ist dann unser Leib ermattet
und mit Blödigkeit begattet,
bald erlieget auch der Geist,
der der Tugend Werkstatt heist.

3. Wer in seines Stands Beruf wandelt auf der
Mittelstrassen,
und kan sich im Essen, Trinken, Schlaffen, Wachen,
Lieben massen,
wird erwünschte Tage leben, ohne Krankheit und
Verdruss
wann er darbet, oder schwebet im beliebten Überfluss.
Also steht in unsrem Händen,
Ungemach von uns zu wenden,
Dann wer Mässigkeit nicht liebt,
niemand mehr als sich betrübt.

Drukkerij „De Hoop" c.v. Zutphen
Chr. F. J. Schriks Pzn.